# COLOR-ONI & CHEESE

# DRAW, DOODLE, USE YOUR NOODLE

### THIS BOOK BELONGS TO

_____

Visit my website at amygreenbank.com

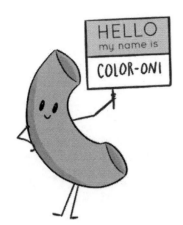

## Hey you, with the crayons!

Before you turn the page, you need to know that this is no ordinary coloring book. The pictures have been started, but it's up to you to fill in the rest.

Color-oni and Cheese will give you ideas to finish the drawings, but remember, you are the artist! So don't be afraid to get crazy!

If you see an empty hamster cage, for example, you could add a hamster. Or you could add a fire breathing dragon. Maybe even a unicorn, alien, or llama.

So go ahead, grab a pencil and get creative.

Your favorite toy maker has asked you to create a new stuffed animal! What will you make?

Artwork By:

_____

# Create the craziest sandwich you can!

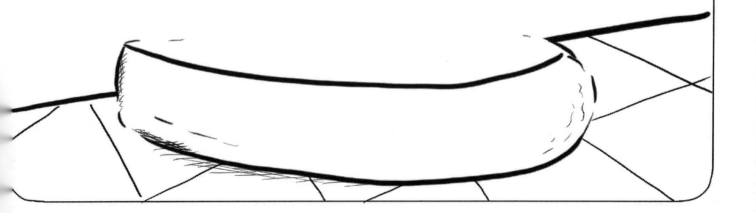

Artwork By:

_____

Oops! You dropped a magic bean! What plant is growing from it?

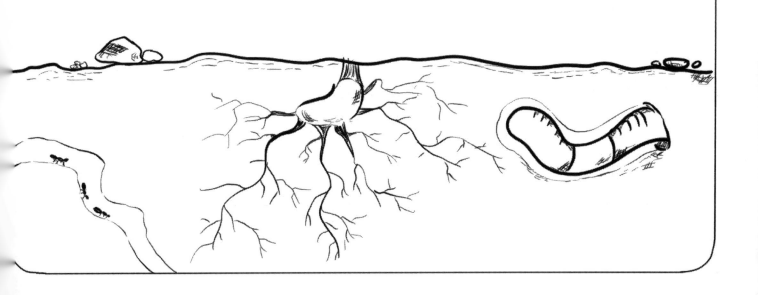

Artwork By:

_____

# Whose wacky hair is this?

Artwork By:

_____

If you could eat any ice cream flavor, what would it be?

Artwork By:

_____

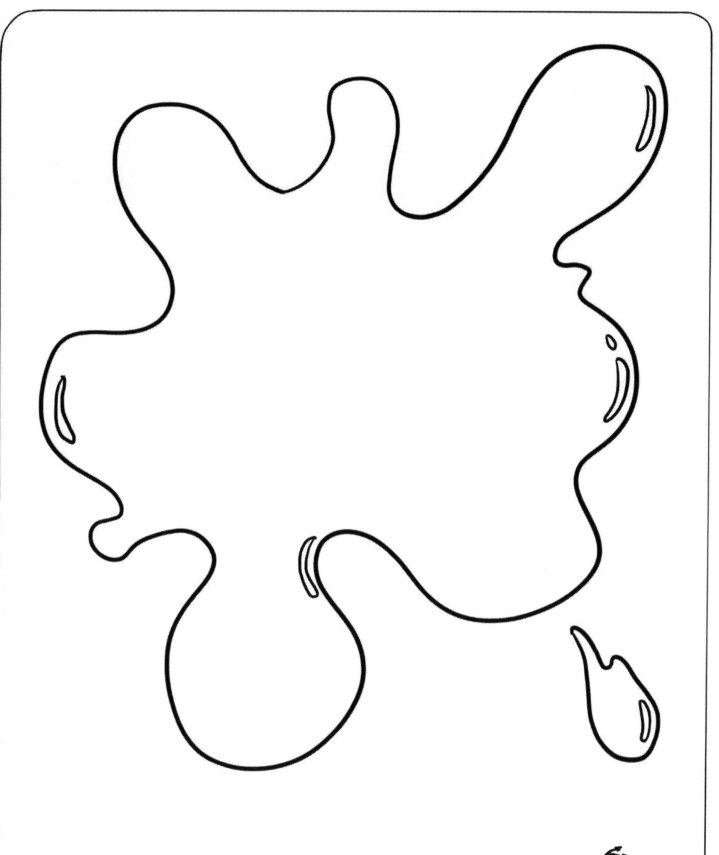

Gross! You dropped your slime behind the couch! What's stuck in the goo?

Artwork By:

_____

What show are these people watching?

Artwork By:

_____

Brr! What's inside the snow globe?

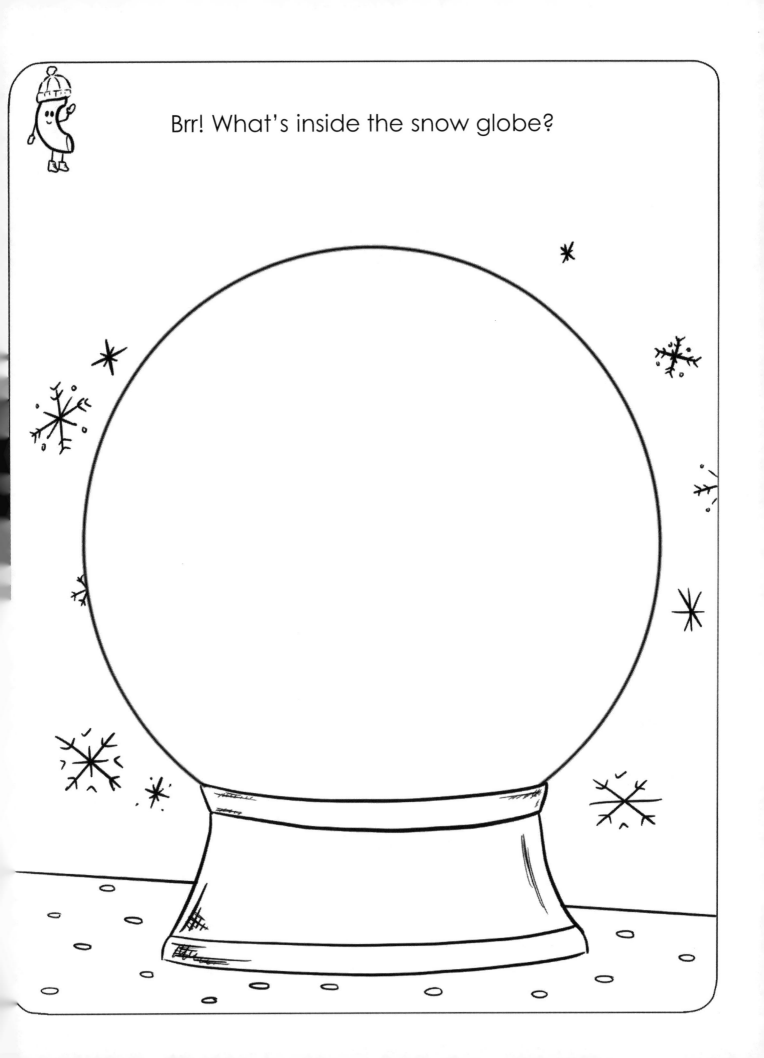

Artwork By:

_____

If you could invent any potato chip flavor,
what would it be?

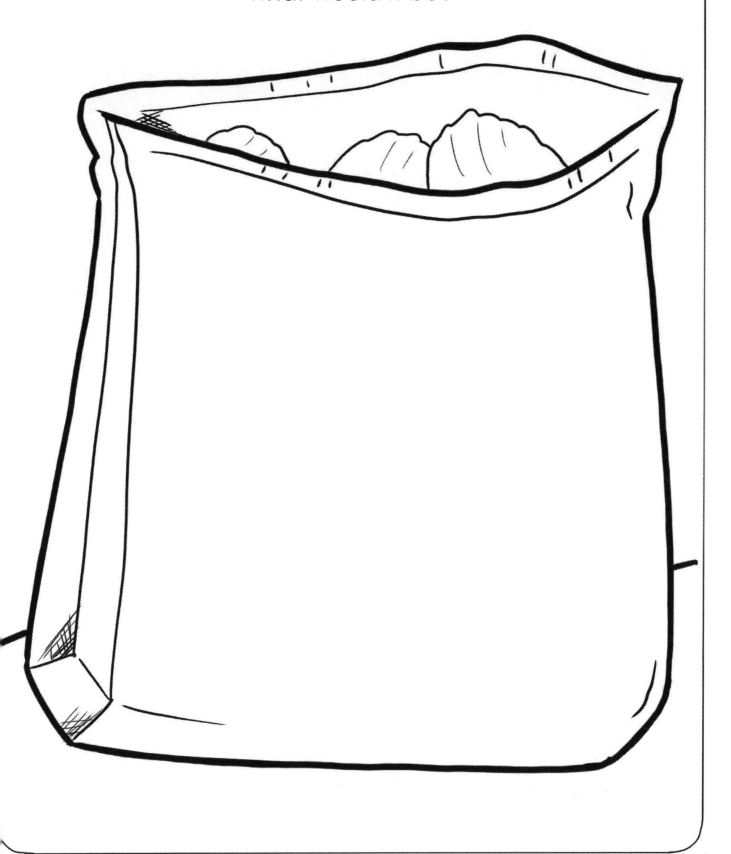

Artwork By:

# Yay! You got a new pet! What is it?

Artwork By:

_____

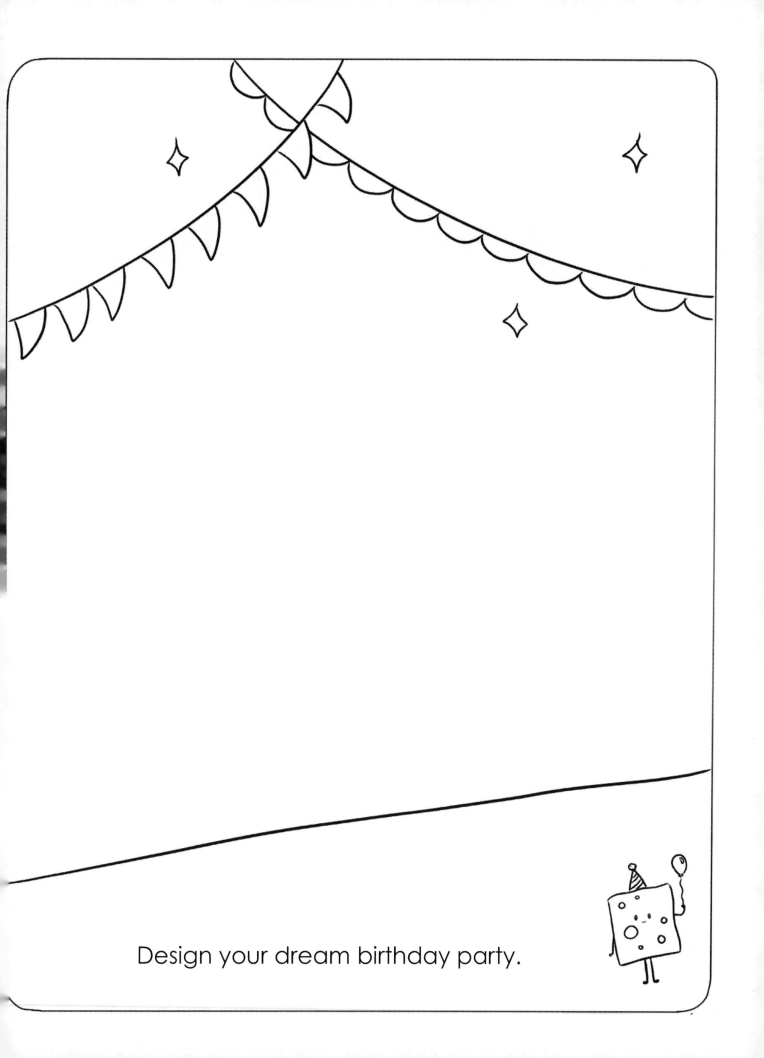

Design your dream birthday party.

Artwork By:

_____

As an underwear designer, you have some big ideas for the world's greatest undies!

Artwork By:

_____

 How about some socks to go with those fancy undies?

Artwork By:

_____

# Who is this kid?

Artwork By:

_____

# Hold on tight! Who is having this magic carpet ride?

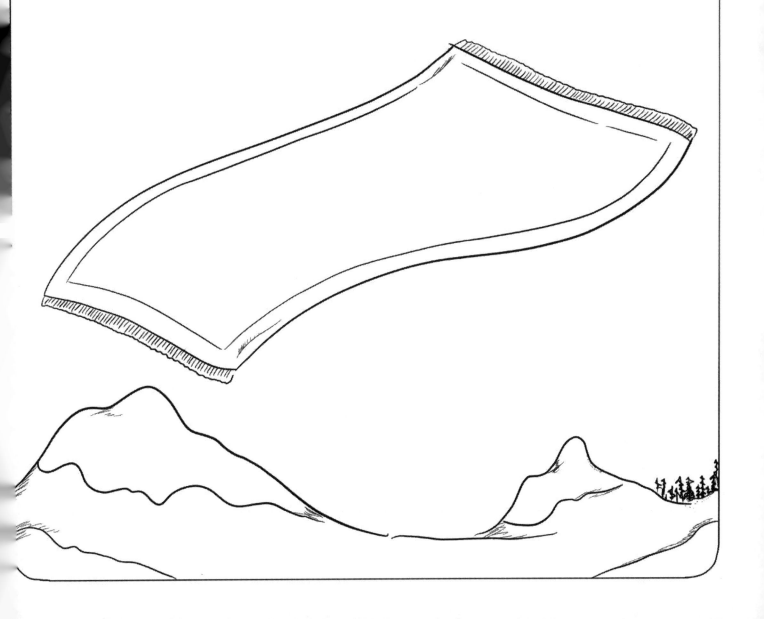

Artwork By:

_____

Time for art class! What will you make?

Artwork By:

_____

# Sweet! Invent some new candies!

Artwork By:

_____

Grab your scissors! Cut out these dinosaur parts and use them to create a new dino on the next page.

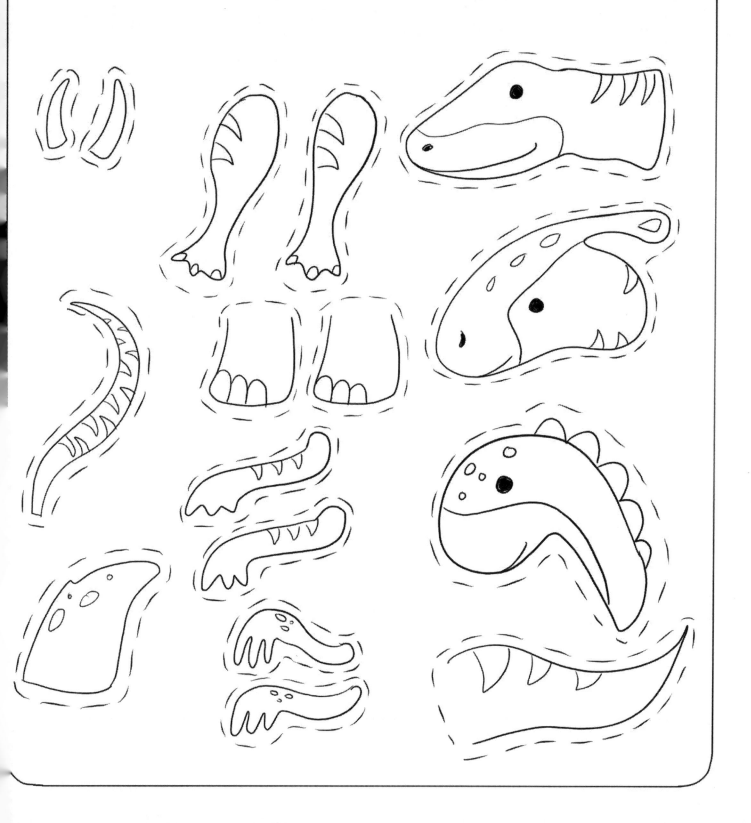

Artwork By:

_____

Glue on the dinosaur parts from the previous page.

Artwork By:

_____

A little peek through your telescope tells you
something strange is going on!
Who is flying this spaceship?

Artwork By:

_____

Finish this clown.

Artwork By:

_____

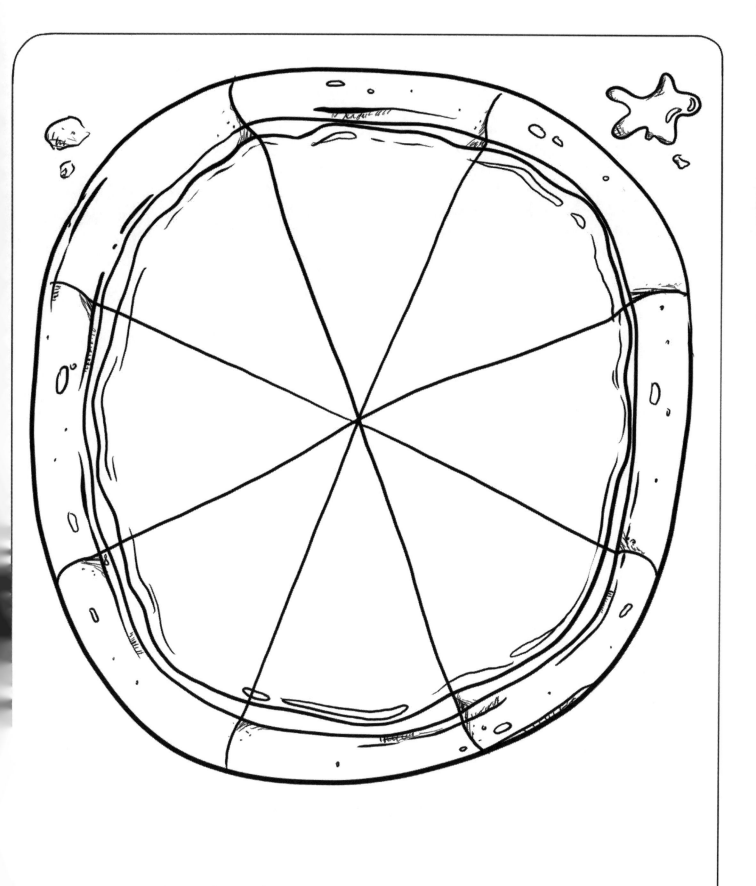

Pizza for dinner! You add the toppings!

Artwork By:

_____

# Design the most amazing waterpark you can imagine.

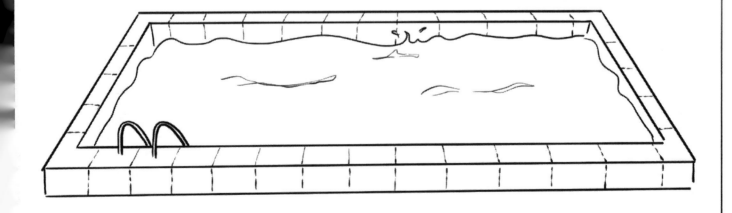

Artwork By:

_____

You've formulated a magical potion. What does it do?

Artwork By:

_____

Yum! Fresh from the oven.
How will you decorate these cookies?

Artwork By:

_____

You've stumbled into this dark, damp cave.
What's in here?

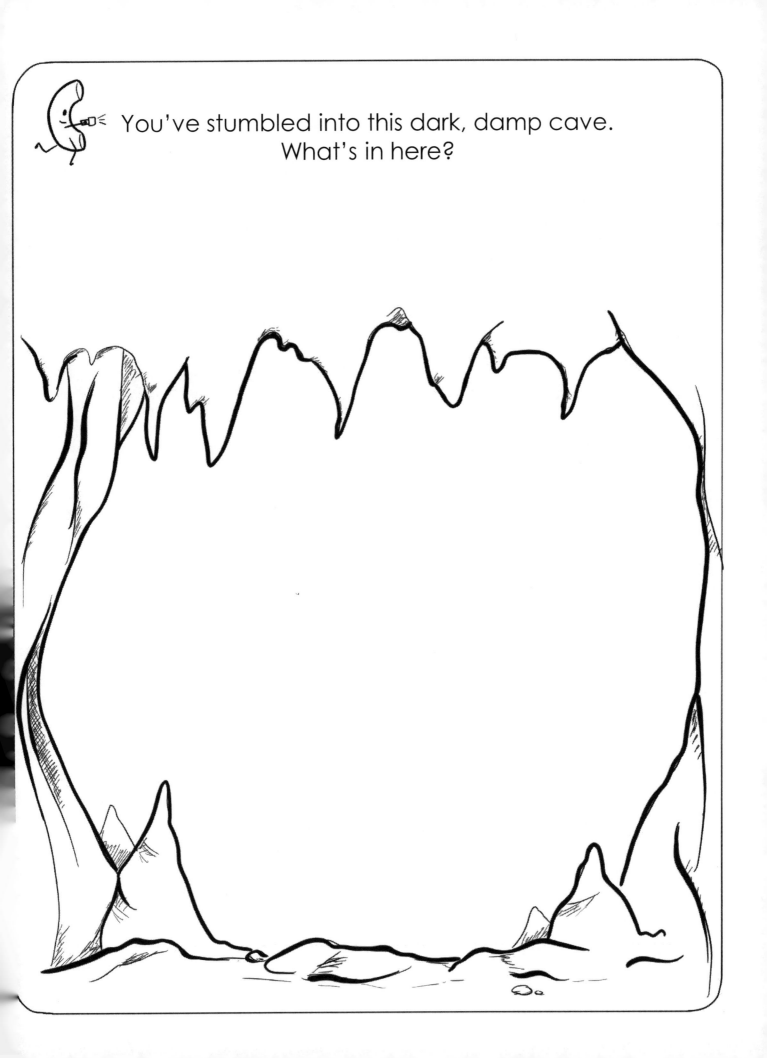

Artwork By:

_____

You've discovered a new kind of insect!
What does it look like?

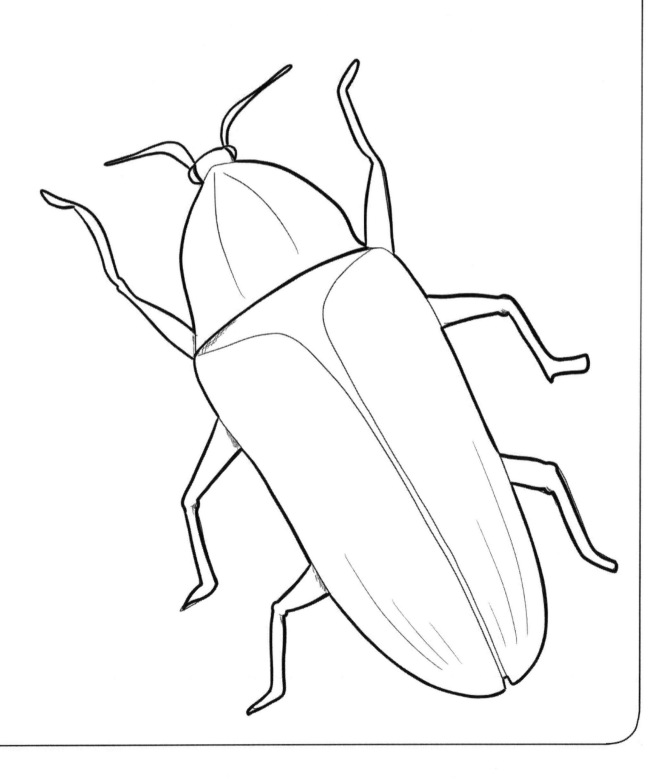

Artwork By:

_____

# Draw a self portrait.

Artwork By:

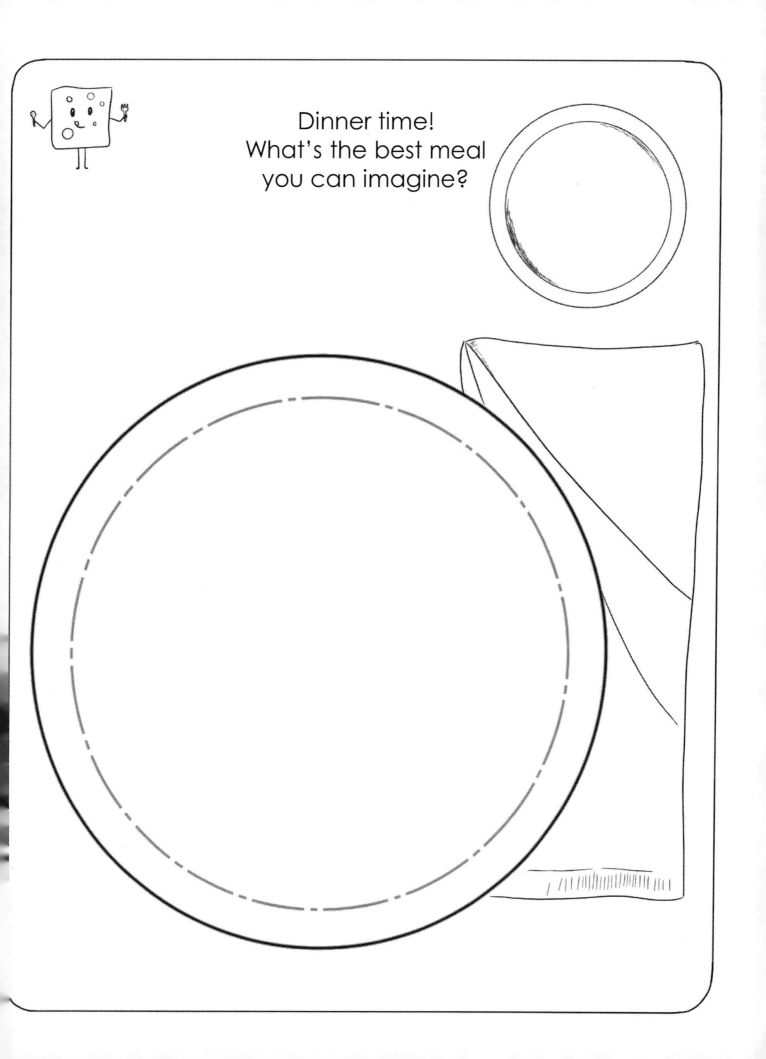

Dinner time!
What's the best meal
you can imagine?

Artwork By:

_____

Splash! Who is holding the umbrella?

Artwork By:

_____

Good Morning! Create a new cereal and design the box.

Artwork By:

_____

# Who flies with these wings?

Artwork By:

_____

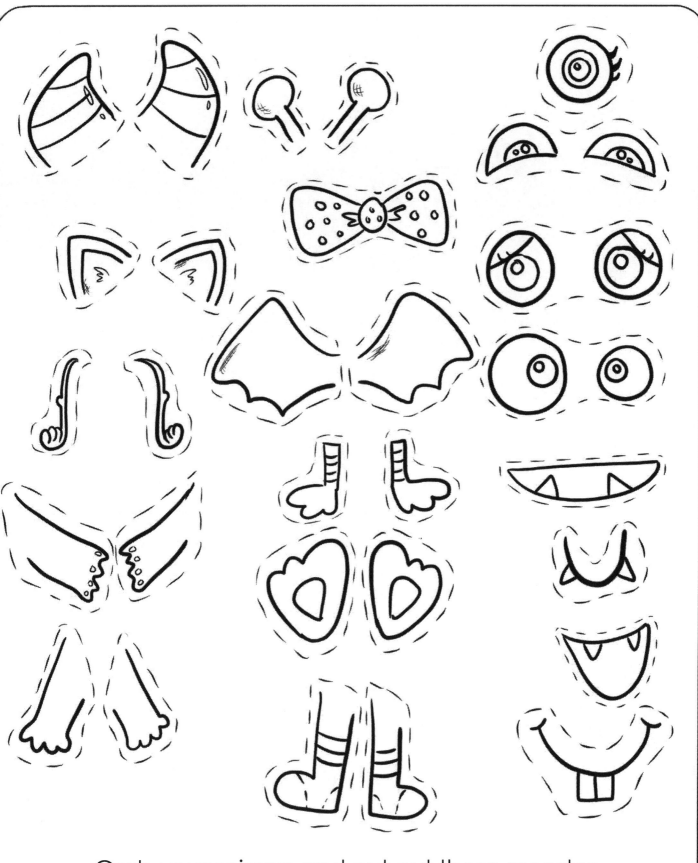

Grab your scissors and cut out these monster parts. Glue them onto the next page to make your own monster!

Artwork By:

_____

 Glue on the monster pieces from the previous page.

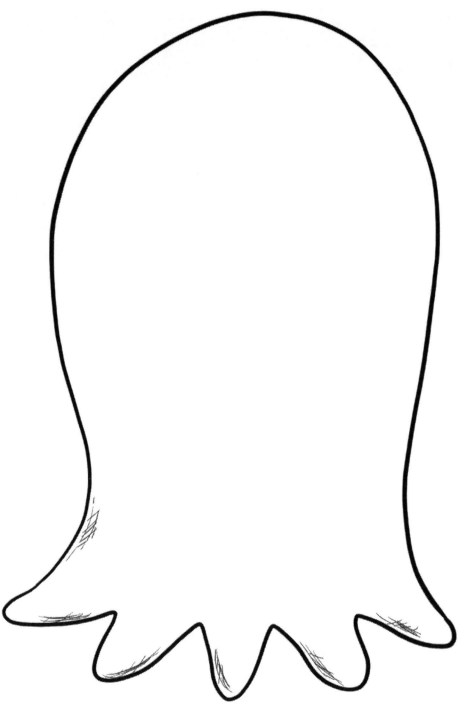

Artwork By:

_____

# Ahoy! Who is on the boat?

Artwork By:

_____

You are on a deep sea adventure! What creatures live here?

Artwork By:

_____

# Happy Birthday! Decorate your cake!

Artwork By:

_____

# What's at the top of the beanstalk?

Artwork By:

_____

# Draw a picture over the puzzle pieces and cut them out.
## Can you put it back together?

Artwork By:

_____

# Decorate your dream bedroom.

Artwork By:

_____

Can you remember your dreams? Draw yourself in the bed and sketch a dream.

Artwork By:

_____

You are a famous author. What is the name
of your book?

Artwork By:

_____

What a beautiful forest. What's here?

Artwork By:

_____

# Whose tail is this?

Artwork By:

_____

Made in the USA
Middletown, DE
25 September 2020